Allow Your Children to
Fail
if You Want Them to
S U C C E E D

DR. AVRIL P. BECKFORD,
PEDIATRICIAN

Bloomington, IN Milton Keynes, UK

authorHOUSE®

AuthorHouse™
1663 Liberty Drive, Suite 200
Bloomington, IN 47403
www.authorhouse.com
Phone: 1-800-839-8640

AuthorHouse™ *UK Ltd.*
500 Avebury Boulevard
Central Milton Keynes, MK9 2BE
www.authorhouse.co.uk
Phone: 08001974150

First published by AuthorHouse 11/9/2006

ISBN: 1-4259-7648-4 (sc)

Library of Congress Control Number: 2006909723

Printed in the United States of America
Bloomington, Indiana

This book is printed on acid-free paper.

Photo by Phyllis, Kandul Photography, Atlanta, GA

Disclosure Statement:
All names (except for family) have been changed, and all true stories modified, so as protect confidentiality and identity. Any resemblance to any name or situation is purely coincidental.

THIS BOOK IS DEDICATED TO:

My parents, Pat and Cyril Beckford, and
my sister, Theresa Bennett,
for their unconditional love;

My husband, Lawrence Rowley MD,
who believed in me and made
the loving journey through parenting;

My sons, Justin and Derek,
whom I love unconditionally and forever;

My patients and their parents, whom
I am honored to serve;

Teachers – the noblest of professionals;

My mentors, Dr. Cheston Berlin, Dr. Bill Fox,
Hampton Morris and Dr. Spencer Gelernter,
who inspired me.

CONTENTS

INTRODUCTION

This book is inspired by my love for children and my belief that every child deserves a chance to succeed. It is about parents partnering with educators to give children the courage to make mistakes, and fail, and learn far more because they did. It is about taking the shame out of failure. It is about seeing failure as a normal part of growth, development and learning. Above all, it challenges parents to lighten up and stop micromanaging and overprotecting, for this creates a barrier to learning, responsibility, accountability and the development of resilience and character.

CHAPTER 1

Failure – You Can't Succeed Without It

Children will only succeed in life if we are brave enough and wise enough to allow them to fail. Many of us learned more from life's bumps in the road than from our successes—especially when we found courage to take a leap or risk and spread our wings and stretch our limits. We cannot raise resilient and resourceful children if we do not allow them to fail and find the courage to stand up again. Edison's inventions changed the world we live in. It was his willingness to risk failure, learn from failure, and start again that resulted in his success. Imagine if his mother had forbidden his efforts for fear that he might fail or be an embarrassment.

Kenneth S. Kosik, MD, professor of neuroscience (and I believe a true legend and visionary in the medical and research fields) believes that making mistakes and the process of problem-solving and working through them are critical to learning and memory.

Why then do I increasingly observe what I call the "bubble wrap syndrome": parents protecting their children from natural consequences, micromanaging their lives—academic, athletic, and social—trying to negotiate their lives to ensure their success? "I want her to feel good about herself. I want to give her a good self-esteem." Self-esteem is not given; it is earned, through hard work and good attitude and the determination and discipline to keep trying even when the successful outcome is not guaranteed.

There are good lessons to be learned from those parents willing to allow their children to stretch and even fail.

Let us raise resilient children. We give them a great gift if we allow them to face challenge and have ownership of their actions. Natural consequence is a great teacher. A life without challenge is a life without character.

Based on twenty years of professional experience, I challenge parents and teachers to allow children to fail to empower them to succeed. I hope to give you practical tools and colorful stories to which you can relate and with which you can identify.

Allow Your Children to Fail if You Want Them to Succeed will be unique in that it will:

- Encourage parents to be comfortable with failure
- Relieve stress in children and schools, which is created by parents who micromanage and are overbearing

- Empower children to take ownership of their actions and accept natural consequence
- Allow children to soar and reach even greater potential because they are free of the fear of failure
- Give parents practical take-home messages with practical applications

----

CHAPTER 2

The Bubble Wrap Syndrome

It is a beautiful day in the park. The playground is alive with laughter, shouting, and constant movement. A wide stone wall, no more than six inches high, defines the area. And Mathew, age three, is balancing on top with his arms spread-eagled, face toward the sun, feeling on top of the world. His mother runs toward him Mathew, stop this instant! You will fall and break your arm. Here, let me lift you down!" She rescues him from his joy. He squirms in protest, but then his three-year-old energy escapes to the slide and he heads immediately in that direction, trying to escape the grip of his mother, who is in hot pursuit. "Mathew, no. That is too tall. You may fall!" Mathew surrenders to her. She directs him to the baby swings, where the eighteen-month-olds are in safety seats. And after quite a struggle he maneuvers his legs through the harness. He straightens his legs and arches his back in frustration, and she thinks, *He will settle down. This is much safer. And after all, all children like swings.* Mathew has learned a subconscious life lesson today:

- Falling must be really bad (whatever falling means).
- Today started off being fun but something pricked the bubble. He used to feel that safe felt good.

Mathew's mother noticed some of the other parents staring at her as she hovered over Mathew. *What would they know about safety? They are much younger mothers than me.* After all, she had waited fifteen years for Mathew and would never let anything happen to him! She arrived home exhausted. Mathew seemed particularly frustrated. *Someday he will understand,* she thought.

In the same park on the same day, Cooper, age three, is running along that same wall. As he runs he calls, " Mommy, look how big I am. What if I fall?" His mother smiles, treasuring how adventurous he is, and answers, "If you fall, I'll be here." Cooper falls. He hops up and dusts his knees as his mother calmly walks over to his side. She smiles and gives him a gentle hug. "You are so brave! Here, let me see you climb that wall again." He scrambles up laughing, running steadily along the wall, a little more cautiously at first but exuberant. Cooper has learned an important lesson in life today:

- When we explore and stretch our limits we may fall. It's not that bad. You just have to be able to get up and try again.

Cooper goes on to explore much of the playground equipment. Some of it he masters; some he doesn't. He is just fine with that. He and his mother return home laughing.

Summer is drawing near. Avery, age twelve, is very excited. Her parents have finally agreed to let her go to camp. Her peers have been attending summer camp for three years now, but her parents have not allowed her to be away from home. There is an orientation meeting scheduled for one of the weekends. The aim is to help campers and parents feel more comfortable.

Of course, Avery's family is the first to arrive and Avery sits next to her mother while the other prospective campers take a seat on the floor, chatting comfortably with each other. The camp director is warm and engaging and outlines the activities for the approaching summer camp, outlining neatly the Health, safety, and nutritional goals. The parents listen attentively and grow more relaxed. At the end of the presentation, the camp director invites questions. Avery's mother stands and removes a long list from her purse. She has been on the Internet researching and researching. She wants every detail in place. She launches forth. Was she even listening before?

"How can I be sure that the cabin counselor is qualified to take care of my daughter?

Can you assure me that she will always have PABA-free sunscreen on at all times?

What precautions are in place for infection control?

Are all camp personnel CPR certified ?

If she is home-sick will you let her call?

What if there is someone in her cabin she does not like?

What guarantees can you give me that she will be safe at all times?"

Avery has mixed emotions. Suddenly camp suddenly sounds like a risky place, yet she longs for a chance to spread her wings and feels her cheeks flushing at her mother's questions, and as she feels the gaze of the other girls upon her.

The camp director smiles a compassionate and warm smile. He has been doing this for twenty years, and even though he has addressed all these topics in reasonable detail in his address, he takes the time to answer because he knows that Avery, more than anyone, needs this camp experience.

"Mrs. Courtney, there are no absolute guarantees in life. I can promise you my commitment to reasonable safety at all times. I can promise you that your daughter will be nurtured and cared for. I will guess, after years of experience, that she will adapt to those in her cabin and grow from the experience. We cannot prevent the usual minor scrapes that come from having fun, unless we wrap the children in bubble-wrap. And we both know that would be no fun."

In a changing world where there are wonderful conveniences that it is easy to take for granted. Our children are sometimes robbed of the character-building challenges that should be part of everyday life. There are many things that parents can actively do to ensure that daily life does include challenge; it is a vital part of raising children who are resilient and resourceful.

The greatest gifts in my life have been:

- I was born to family of very modest means.
- I had great parents who
    - Taught me to love and respect everyone
    - Taught me love and respect for a higher power
    - Held me accountable for my actions
    - Provided a nurturing environment without overprotecting me
    - Loved me unconditionally with love that never depended on my performance
    - Cared more about what kind of person I was than about what I achieved
    - Treasured education and educators

My early childhood memories are ones of adventure and exploration, because that's the kind of girl I was. The advantages of growing up in a small town with parents who had good common sense were enormous.

We played outside a lot. Organized team sports for little children were not part of the culture. How important those opportunities for life's lessons were. We had to learn to play fair and be nice or our peers would enforce that natural consequence rule: "We don't want to play with you anymore. You need to sit out" This is far more effective than having the constant micromanagement of a coach at age five. Parents would supervise from a healthy distance, encouraging us to resolve our own little issues but always being available to intercede or nurture as needed.

Living in a small town, my parents nurtured my independence. As early as eight I road my bicycle to the post office (about two miles away) to deposit my weekly savings (five cents) and to the store to buy lettuce for my rabbit and guinea pig. It was made perfectly clear to me that I had the responsibility of caring for them fully. I also cycled to the local tennis club, where I spent hours practicing against the tennis wall. Private coaching was not in the budget and certainly not the norm for any of the children, unless they first showed the commitment to practice and hard work of their own . This is a far cry from what I observe today: children overscheduled and over-coached in sports, dance, music, whether or not they show any interest or passion. Sadly the surest way to decrease motivation is for parents to pressure their children into fulfilling the parents' own dreams. Passion has to come from within; it has to be nurtured and supported.

So then, times have changed—especially if families live in larger metropolitan areas. This kind of independence is not always safe or practical in those areas. There are solutions. For example, my husband and I sought out vacation venues that would encourage such opportunities. At one of our favorite beech resorts, the children could ride their bicycles on private roads to the local post office, fishing pier, and ice-cream store beginning at an early age. Their independence and the time allowed was gradually increased as they got older and demonstrated the appropriate levels of responsibility. Even packing for vacation becomes a wonderful opportunity for learning and growth and organizational skills. At two, it was more like a game. Together we placed socks, T-shirts, and the like into separate piles together. Then gradually we advanced to lists that we checked off together and ultimately to packing on your own. The sense of ownership and choice and responsibility does wonders for building self-esteem, rather than having Mom or Dad do it all for you.

Some take-home messages for avoiding the bubble-wrap syndrome:

TAKE-HOME MESSAGES

- Safety without neurosis is healthy. (The Academy of Pediatrics has excellent guidelines for healthy safety.)
- It is okay to fall. Teach your children to stand up again
- Don't do daily chores for your children that they could do for themselves. Independence and responsibility build self -esteem.
- Set the limits and then let your children have fun within those boundaries.
- Learn to laugh at yourself when you blunder. You will be giving your children a great gift and lesson in life.
- Don't try to be the perfect parent. There is nothing worse for a child than living with perfection: the kind of parent not strong enough to be vulnerable, acknowledge his or her mistakes, and try again.

CHAPTER 3

Under-Nurtured, Overindulged

Jeffrey is nine. He wakes up to the alarm clock and rubs his eyes. No good morning hug. He tugs at his clothes for the school day. He wears the same socks as yesterday and a rumpled T-shirt, but both are expensive—designer stuff that the other kids think is cool. Oh well. Mom must have been too busy again. She mentioned that she had a major business presentation. He wanders downstairs and finds one of the four cereal boxes in the cupboard still has some cereal and he has his breakfast. There is a Post-It note on the table with a ten dollar bill: *No time to fix lunch. Buy whatever you want. Mom.* There is a smiley-face drawn next to the word *mom.* Funny, that's not how he feels. Well at least he can buy soda, potato chips, and candy for lunch. The other kids always say "You are so lucky!" Funny, he didn't really feel that way. Jeffrey ambles out, feet dragging, to the bus stop. It's chilly. He didn't know that it would be, but there's no time to turn back. He'll have to face Mrs. Williams again in the classroom. "What, Jeffrey? No sweater again!" That is always a bad start to the day. As Jeffrey waits for the bus, Albert wanders up, smiling. He turns, waves goodbye to his father, who gives him a proud thumbs-up sign. Albert's dad walks toward the bus stop, a healthy distance away from Albert. Then he holds back, allowing Albert to feel the independence of the last half block. Albert's clothes are hand-me-downs, but they are crisp and clean and he is warm and cozy in his sweater, as his Dad had noted the chill in the air.

Albert can't wait for the end of the day. He and his dad are going to the second-hand sports store to see if there is a baseball bat that is the right size and the right price. He's not sure whether he can make it through the day; he is so excited. He and his dad play a lot together. He has earned half the value of the bat by doing chores around the house and in the neighborhood, and he has watched the big old glass jar gradually fill up. They visited the store once before, but his total was just shy of what he needed. Dad had given him a big hug and an understanding smile and said, "We'll have to come back when we have earned a little extra." It had been a bit disappointing, but he was even more excited now. He could see every detail of that bat in his head, as he had pictured it every night. He could smell it and feel it in his hand, and he could imagine himself hitting the ball out of the park with it. He could also imagine the look on his dad's face when he did, because he knew that no matter what, his dad would be there. His dad wouldn't be the coach (thank goodness), yelling at him and expecting too much. Instead his dad would quietly watching from the side, enjoying every minute. He knew that the only expectation that his dad had of him was that he try hard and have a good attitude, and he loved his dad very much. He knew he never wanted to let him down.

Jeffrey remembers that his mom told him they'd stop by the Pro-Sports store after school and that he could "pick out any bat he wanted" on his way to his private coaching. He's not excited somehow. Mom may not show up if her business presentation goes on too long, and baseball was his folks' idea anyway. He knows that it will be one of those rushed afternoons when they dash into the store and Mom gets impatient with the store attendant. She'll tell him she doesn't really mind what the bat costs, but she'll ask him to please to process things quickly, as she is a very busy woman. Then she'll drop Jeffrey off at his private batting lesson, reminding him that since she is investing so much time and effort, she hopes this season will yield better results than before. He wishes that he could tell her that it is comments like that that race through his head as he gets up to bat and then everything inside his head freezes and he can't remember all those things the coach wants him to remember. It is usually complicated by his father yelling "Hit the ball!" and at the same time the exasperated voice of the coach yells "What are you swinging for? That was a ball, not a strike!" It's worse when they bring Grandma and Grandad to that one game of the year and remind him of how the grandparents are expecting "a good performance." Jeffery always wonders why Albert is always smiling and swings hard, and isn't afraid to strike out. He seems to have so much fun. He likes Albert. He wishes he could go home to Albert's house just once, though his parents say "We don't like the neighborhood." What is that supposed to mean? It must be a pretty fine place for Albert to be so happy.

Children respond so beautifully to a simple nurturing environment. Today parents all too often substitute stuff for time and love. Everyday I see both younger and older children ruined by what I think is a syndrome of under-nurturing and overindulgence. Parents confuse encouragement with pressure. Some simple take-home messages are:

TAKE-HOME MESSAGES

- All children and adolescents should wake up to a warm "good-morning" from a caring adult. No child should start his or her school day alone, without breakfast and a hug.
- All children and adolescents should return from school to an environment where a caring adult asks them about their day. (This may be a parent, caregiver, after-school-program, Boys and Girls Club, or a neighbor.) No child should come home on a regular basis to a key under the doormat, an empty refrigerator, and the television and Internet as a babysitter.
- All children and adolescents should be encouraged to participate, not pressured to perform.
- All children and adolescents should have the right to unconditional love that does not depend on performance.
- All children and adolescents should have their basic material needs met (food, clothing, school supplies, medical needs) and should be encouraged to earn (even in small ways) things that might be considered luxuries (for example, upgrades on sports equipment).
- All children and adolescents should be encouraged to be responsible. Allow your children to do for themselves things that they are capable of doing.

CHAPTER 4

Parents - The Most Important Gift You Can Give Your Children!

"Things which matter the most must never be at the mercy of things that matter the least." - Goethe

Ponder for a moment: What is really important to you? Choose three things around which your life revolves. Imagine that this is your legacy - the things by which you will be judged and remembered when you are long gone.

Ponder again what percentage of this day, this week, this month, this year you allocated in real time to these things. What was the quality of the time you devoted to these things? Most importantly, how many opportunities did you miss to make a difference?

Over the years as I speak with parents and colleagues, though the priorities are varied, there lies a common thread in terms of what's important. Those who are meeting the challenge of parenting and a profession commonly identify as most important things in varying order:

family, religious conviction, and career. Others included health and recreational pursuits. What was interesting is that when I ask whether time commitment or the investment of emotional energy matched the order of priority, the answer was most often no.

For those of us who aspire to become good parents, it seems to me that the first thing we have to do is TO TAKE CHARGE OF OUR OWN LIVES, investing not only the time but the emotional energy appropriately into parenting.

Parenting is the most important and the most difficult thing we will ever do. I am convinced that it is not only impossible but unwise to be perfect parents, and I found great peace personally when I was able to accept this. How else will our children learn to make mistakes, forgive themselves, and start again if they don't see this modeled? Parents who work both outside and inside the home face an extra challenge in setting priorities.

As a pediatrician married to an obstetrician-gynecologist. I finally realized that working hard to find more flexibility and time for my family would not compromise my standards of medical practice (provided I had equally committed partners with whom to work) and it would definitely bring me closer to reaching my ideals as a parent. I subsequently founded my own practice and built it up to an eight-person group—all outstanding and hardworking but committed to a balance in life. My husband shares this commitment and is a very active and equal partner in parenting.

At a conference that I lead entitled "The Challenge of Combining Parenting and Profession," one of the pediatricians made the very important point that we all pass through "seasons" in our lives. Depending on those stages (seasons), the time allocated to different priorities must and will vary.

After many years of carefully observing parent-child interaction, I am absolutely convinced that *it is the little things that mean the most to children in their social-emotional development.* It is stating the obvious and giving those little practical reassurances that lays the foundation for security and the first building blocks of self-esteem.

Every moment is precious.

Even the little act of changing a diaper is a wonderful opportunity and privilege not only to provide comfort and nurturing but to have a positive social interaction: Don't see this precious moment as a chore. Think about it:

We convey with our body language:

You are important to me.

I am attuned to what you need.

You are loved and safe.

I lovingly caress you.

You make me happy; see how I smile.

From infancy our children see themselves in the mirror we reflect back to them: That mirror is our tone of voice, our body language, our presence, our emotional connectedness and attunement. We should not allow our own stress or overcrowded schedules to interfere with those precious moments of interaction. It always amazes me and saddens me how often children subconsciously hold themselves responsible for their parents' mood or behavior: "If only I was a little better maybe Mom and Dad wouldn't fight." "They wouldn't have got divorced if I wasn't so bad." "I don't seem to be able to make my dad happy."

I believe that we can be successful parents and successful professionals if we make parenting our priority.

If we did not wake up tomorrow, however successful we are professionally, there would be someone to fill our shoes in our professional life. There is no one who could ever quite fill our unique role as Mom or Dad. The way we prioritize impacts not only our own lives but the lives of those most precious to us. Sometimes what seems like an unimportant little event at the start of our day may set the tone for the entire day for our child, and sometimes it may set the tone for much more of his or her future.

Gavin and Frances are two very successful attorneys in a major city. They went to highly reputable law schools and are partners in highly reputable law firms. Of course, they wanted their children to attend the best independent school (based on the community opinion of who's who), though the educational consultant with whom they met advised another outstanding school because she felt it would be a good match for their child. As Gavin was driving up the long driveway to the preschool, his cell phone rang and he answered it immediately (as he always did). He focused on this call from work as he pulled up to the curb where the headmistress was waiting to greet each of the children and their parents by name. He nodded at her and shot a quick farewell glance at his daughter Katie. *Multitasking,* he thought to himself and gave himself a self-congratulatory mental pat on the back, suppressing that annoying fleeting thought that Katie didn't seem quite happy. *She must be happy. She has everything,* he thought momentarily as he resumed his conversation. Katie had wanted to tell him about the butterflies in her tummy, because today she was supposed to find her coat-hanger herself and hang her book-bag and coat there. The problem was it had to be at the spot marked with a yellow triangle. She could remember the color yellow but she couldn't remember the triangle shape. She had hoped to ask her Dad in the car, but he was on the cell phone and she knew better than to interrupt when he was talking to someone at the office. Only once had she told him that she had a problem with shapes and he looked angry and disappointed and said he would get a tutor. She was only four and she didn't know what a tutor was, but she sure knew she needed a hug. She ventured down the hall, which seemed longer today, and saw the yellow and lunged at it, tossing her coat and book-bag onto the hook. Almost at the same second she heard Emily squeal, "Dummy! Don't you know that's the yellow rectangle. That's not yours!" She was so startled and embarrassed that she gave Emily a gentle shove, just in time to be seen by Mrs. Robinson. Mrs. Robinson made her sit in time-out for shoving, but Emily didn't get to sit in time-out for calling names. This was a no-good-very-bad day. When her father picked her up at the curb at the end of the day (and was on the cell phone again), she was pouting angrily with her arms crossed. As he continued his phone conversation he thought, *I'll call the very best child psychologist today and have her seen immediately.*

Katie was thinking about her friend Tessa and how she had laughed and played today. Her daddy was also a partner in the same law firm, but here was how Tessa's day had started: As Tessa's dad was driving up to carpool, his cell phone rang, and he recognized the caller as his boss—the managing partner of his law firm: "Hello, John. May I call you back in a few minutes? I'm in the middle of important time with my daughter Tessa. Thank you for understanding." Tessa felt a warm and fuzzy feeling in her tummy. She was also relieved because today they had to hang their coats on the coat-hanger with the right color and shape. Hers was the purple circle and she always confused the oval and the circle. "Daddy, how can I remember the circle for today?" He made the circle shape with his left thumb and forefinger and said "Look, it is round, no beginning and no end. It just goes on and on, just like my love for you!" She would never forget the circle. She threw her little arms around her daddy's neck and went skipping into school, placing her coat confidently on the correct coat-hanger marked with a purple circle. She paused only to help a friend debating over the oval shape. She was so happy; she felt she could do anything and help anyone. Meanwhile, in the car, her father returned the call to the managing partner, John. John, initially a little irritated at being deferred for family reasons answered the phone warmly, for the moment had given him pause—time to reflect on how much he respected that Tessa's father's priorities were firmly intact, and time to wish that he hadn't missed those opportunities in his younger days.

TAKE-HOME MESSAGES

1. Make parenting a top priority and work to allow professions to accommodate this need.
2. Don't overprotect your children: Challenge, taking responsibility for our own behavior, and earning what we achieve are essential to the development of good character.
3. Take charge of technology. Make it serve your family needs rather than intrude upon it.
4. Who we are and what we do, rather than what we say, have the greatest impact on your children's behavior.

5. Take a stand on ethical issues and try to live that way. Allow room for human error. Let your child know that you too are human and vulnerable, and that realizing it is a strength.
6. Less is more. Give less stuff and more love.
7. It is the little things that mean a lot.
8. BE THERE emotionally and physically through good times and tough times. Let your children know that your love is unconditional.

CHAPTER 5

Stress - Help Your Child to Cope

Stress is part of life. Though we cannot shield our children from stress, it is essential that we give them the tools to recognize it, cope with it, and avoid unnecessary exposure to it. One of our most important roles as parents is to raise our children to be good human beings who are emotionally intelligent and can cope with life and contribute to society in a positive way.

One of the most common causes of stress is parents! Parents can cause enormous stress by their absence (physically and emotionally) and by their overbearing presence: micromanaging every aspect of their child's life. With the divorce rate over fifty percent, single parenting is common, and not without challenge. More devastating, however, are the parents who are physically present but emotionally absent because of being stressed, overwhelmed, depressed, or just too self-absorbed with their own goals, wants, or needs to be able to do their most important job: to nurture their child, who is growing up in a stressful environment. It is the daily consistencies in a child or teen's life that gives him or her that emotional security and resilience: knowing that that one "safe" person will be there for him or her no matter what. Children need a predictable, savvy, warm, and loving adult. Too many children like Christopher come home to an empty house after a tough day in the locker room, and when his mom comes home, instead of being able to let it all out, he has the added worry of whether she'll be in a good mood or whether it will be one of those many tear-filled (or worse still) volatile afternoons when he can do no right. When his defenses are already down, will she shower him with a barrage of questions about his grades and performance and remind him how he'll "end up like his father—a good-for-nothing loser"? Today of all days, a sandwich and hot chocolate would have been nice. Instead he carries the additional burden of his mother's stress and the responsibility of his and her future on his shoulders. No wonder he has moments when he wants to try something to help him "forget it all," or worse still, when he wonders if it is worth being around at all. Amy desperately needed a hug because her excellent grades "aren't cool" and today her peers let her know many times "how weird" she is because she studies hard and "simply has no idea about what shoes are in and what shoes are out." Her mom was on the cell phone from the time she picked Amy up from school until they were in their house. She was closing a real estate deal. "So that you can attend a decent college," she justifies herself to Amy. For the first time, Amy is thinking "Maybe there won't even be a college. Maybe I'll just stop studying and drop my grades. Maybe then you'll notice me and talk—I mean really talk to me." One of the most important things parents can do is deal with their own stress.

There are many causes of parental stress—some day-to-day and relatively minor, and some major. How we handle our own stress serves as a model for our own children. If we are reluctant to seek help or to acknowledge our stress and deal constructively with it, we send a powerful message to our children.

The "cold war" marriage, for example, wherein hostility and the absence of laughter fill the air, can be destructive to children; they feel responsible.

Change is yet another form of stress. Change of address, occupation, school, friends, birth of a sibling, illness in a family member, divorce, all represent significant stress. This is exacerbated by the news, whether it be television, newspapers or magazines. Bad news sells, and children and adolescents can become overwhelmed with a sense of the world falling apart around them.

Competition has become part of everyday life—competition in sports, academics, and socially. While playing "good enough" and taking part should be celebrated, many parents want their child to "win." They fail to realize that crossing the finish line first is not synonymous with winning. Winning is feeling a sense of accomplishment —achieving a personal goal and having the character to celebrate the success of others.

Over-stimulation represents a major form of stress for children today. Children have very little down time and many grow up with the expectation that they should be constantly entertained. In adolescence and adulthood there is the notion that quiet time for physical and mental nourishment is something foreign that has to be learned, or that it may even evoke bizarre feelings of guilt when not being constantly productive. It would serve our children well not to constantly entertain them. We should help them celebrate quiet time as a time to feel the grass beneath their toes and a time to stop and hear the birds sing.

Lack of social justice is a more subtle and yet powerful form of stress. If children grow up knowing that justice is truth and that ultimately the truth will prevail, they develop a sense of security and comfort when doing what is right. Even in this wonderful country, the home of democracy and respect for the rights of the individual, all too often children learn that legal outcomes depend not always on the truth but on the oratory, skill, and yes, the cost of the legal counsel. We have to keep hope alive and work toward a justice system that gives a wayward teenager from a financially and socially challenged environment the same access to excellent representation as the corporate wizards and celebrities. If children live with a sense of justice, they live with a sense of security and are inspired to contribute positively.

Yet another form of stress facing children today is the relative absence of extended family and consistent neighborhoods. The world has become an international community, which has great advantages, but there is a potential downside. Families often move numerous times for professional and other reasons, not only within cities but across states, countries, and continents. This means that whereas children are learning flexibility and adaptability, they are also struggling with not having enough time to plant their roots. Grandparents and significant others are less available to give those needed hugs to both children and their parents during the good and the tough times. The more well-adjusted adults in our children's lives, the better adjusted they will be. When professional or personal pursuits take us away from extended family, it is wise for us to recognize the challenge and proactively do something about it.

My husband, Lawrence, and I settled in the USA and became parents nine thousand miles away from our very treasured families. We realized early on (and increasingly with time) that our children were missing out on something very special: the hands-on nurturing of grandparents' unconditional love, the fun to be had, and life's lessons to be learned from close interactions with cousins, aunts, and uncles. We made two important decisions.

The first was to make it possible for our families to visit us in the States and for us to travel back home as often as possible. Moreover, we committed to cherish every moment together.

The second decision was to "adopt" a local family: babysitters, friends, schoolteachers—all of whom enriched our lives enormously.

The effort, organization, and finances involved in making time to be with extended family is negligible in comparison to the emotional rewards that have been reaped. The social-emotional growth of our sons that came from the connectedness of family during these rare but treasured times was extraordinary.

And now for the more difficult but very important second task: adopting a family. John Dunn wrote "No man is an island, entire of itself…." We are all products of those with whom we come in contact . Whether and how we choose to seize the moment and what we learn from every human interaction (positive and negative) affects ultimately who we are and what we become.

I treasure those who reached beyond their defined roles and extended themselves to become part of our family: teachers, childcare-givers, friends, and mentors. My husband is a busy obstetrician and gynecologist and I am a pediatrician. With our demanding professional commitments, it was essential to us that when we were not at home, our children were cared for by people who were genuinely invested in their lives. We helped accomplish this by genuinely investing in the lives of these "extended family members" emotionally, personally, and financially. There was "Ma," the early childhood caregiver with whom my oldest son, Justin, bonded. She picked apples and sang with him. They spent much time together from birth through age two. After we moved we maintained contact throughout even the teen years, journeying back to Pennsylvania. We did this to show our appreciation and help my son learn the important message that we are all a product of those who touch our lives. There was Lucy, my youngest son's early caregiver, who nurtured him and gave him so much love and affection and laughter. Expression of affection is extremely important to me, and it meant a great deal to see Lucy responding with warmth and affection too. This warmth and comfort with affection became an intrinsic part of their nature.

Then there was Amanda, a teacher working on her masters' degree in early childhood development, who knew the importance of play, of laughter, of love, of tears and of patience and down time. When she married, my boys were the ring-bearers in her wedding at ages six and four. This was a special day and we all treasure the memory. As the bride reached the alter, Justin, age six, stopped and said in a very audible stage whisper; "Amanda, you look so beautiful. I just wish it was me marrying you!" The relationship continues years later, and now as teens, my boys have visited a number of times to help Amanda out with her own children—a treasured adopted family.

The relationships we have formed throughout the years with the teachers at the boys' extraordinary schools have been unique and very much part of their lives. These positive role models who have invested in them as young men (and not merely as students) have been pivotal in their development. Parents would do well to realize that teachers can be the best partners in helping us raise children of character.

A practical word about childcare-givers—some golden rules for making the right choice: Entrusting the care of your child to anyone for any time at all—whether for a moment or a day—is an important decision. Be sure you invest the time, care, and attention this deserves.

I have been personally blessed with good caregivers and am grateful. Nonetheless, there are many lessons along the way. As a pediatrician I have seen many consequences of caregiver experiences, some good and some unfortunately tragic.

The choice of caregiver is not a simple choice, and you will have to decide what is right for your family. There are a few golden rules that I feel should not be broken:

1. The only worthy caregiver is one who loves and respects children and wants to be a caregiver for exactly that reason. Any other reason for caring

for children (financial, for example) is simply not good enough.

2. You must have an instinctive rapport with the caregiver of your child. If any questions are met with defensiveness, it should raise a red flag.

3. Pay attention not only to the physical safety of your child, but to the emotional nurturing you feel he or she will receive. The caregiver needs to have the time, patience, energy, and the desire to play , laugh, and connect—all with love for your child.

CHAPTER 6

Recipe for Success

I. DON'T MAKE EXCUSES
2. DON'T NEGOTIATE YOUR CHILD'S FUTURE

In order for children to succeed in life, they have to be accountable. In order to be accountable, they have to have ownership of their actions. The surest way for parents to undermine this process is to make excuses for behaviors or outcomes. By making excuses parents rob their child of a great gift: taking responsibility. Since this is one of the foundation stones for building character and self-esteem, making excuses (as opposed to holding our children responsible for their actions) robs them of something precious.

It starts early. Let me differentiate between understanding the emotion behind the behavior and making excuses for the behavior.

Hannah is two years old and her mother is checking out at the cash register. She leans over and grabs a piece of candy, to which her mother responds "no" and places the candy back on the rack. In frustration, she throws a tantrum with all the gusto she can find, kicking and screaming "CANDY!" and turning purple with indignation, all the while fueled by the attention she is getting. (Two-year-olds, after all, would rather get negative attention than no attention at all.) The shop attendant says "Ah, poor little thing." The old lady behind her mother offers awful advice: "It's just a candy. Let her have just this one," while the librarian (who has no children) impatiently waiting at the back says "What children today need is more spankings!" This mother is wise. Despite the fact that she is facing pressure, she understands the emotion behind the behavior and faces the truth squarely: The emotion is frustration. The reason for the frustration is Hannah is not getting what she wants. The mother calmly completes the transaction with the teller, ignores the inappropriate unsolicited advice, and exits promptly with Hannah, placing her firmly in her car seat, without the candy and paying no attention to her wails of protest. This is how things would have gone if Hannah's mother was an excuse-maker. As soon as Hannah started to have her tantrum when the candy was removed, her mother would have worried more about what people around were thinking and made moves to compensate for Hanna's behavior: " She is so tired! She never acts this way otherwise." (This is not true. Hanna may be tired, but tantrums are a normal part of two-year-old behavior and if Hannah is normal, she has likely tested the waters before. How we handle tantrums or protests determines the outcome of future tantrums.) " I am going to give you this candy just this once, if you stop crying." She would speak at a higher volume than necessary and share her eye contact not only with Hannah, but especially with the audience. Hannah, a normal two-year-old who is a concrete thinker at a very important phase of social development, has just learned the following lessons: If I don't get what I want, I kick and scream. When I kick and scream, Mommy gives me what I want. What you and I observe is a bit more: Hannah's mom cares a lot about what others think—at the expense of setting clear limits for Hannah. Extrapolated to the teen and pre-teen years, this is a very unhealthy message to be sending.

There is a world of difference between understanding the emotion behind a behavior and making excuses for that behavior.

Simple courtesy and good manners have to be actively taught and role-modeled. They are the ABCs of showing respect to others during daily interaction. Sadly, many parents think that courtesy is passively acquired. In order to help our children succeed in life and become thoughtful and contributing members of society, teaching them to treat others as they would like to be treated and teaching them to respect boundaries is essential. They otherwise learn that they are at the center of the world—that all else revolves around them. And we are entirely to blame. Annabelle is three. She is in the pediatric office for a checkup and her mother is thoughtfully going through a list of questions with the pediatrician. The adults are actively involved in an important discussion. Annabelle twirls into the middle of the floor, squealing " Look at me, look at me! See how clever I am. Watch me twirl!" Her mother stops mid-sentence, applauds, and joins in with a squeal: "Isn't she wonderful, doctor? She has such great self-esteem!" The scenario repeats itself, and at the third attempt, when Annabelle's mother finally says ever so apologetically to Annabelle " Annabelle, sweetie, let us not interrupt. We are here for your check up," Annabelle has a total meltdown, leading to more cajoling by her mom and the apology that makes mom responsible for Annabelle's behavior. "I'm sorry. doctor. She wouldn't have had the meltdown if I had just let her do the twirl. I guess I hurt her feelings." Looking in from the outside, it may seem simple.

1. Annabelle has learned that she is the center of the room, if not the world.
2. Annabelle has learned that she can set the agenda and the timetable.
3. Annabelle has learned that interrupting adults at any time is fine.
4. Annabelle has learned that melting down (especially publicly) will evoke the necessary angst and compensatory response from her mother.

5. Annabelle's mother has mistaken misdirected confidence for self-esteem.

Here is the teaching moment: When Annabelle first takes her position in the center of the room and squeals, her mother calmly and firmly says "Annabelle, you are interrupting. When we are finished you may demonstrate your twirl." Annabelle has two choices: One, she takes her seat quietly, receiving a warm smile and gentle squeeze on her hand to reaffirm her behavior. Two, she has a meltdown, in which case neither the mother nor pediatrician give attention to the negative behavior and continue their conversation. There are so many little opportunities for helping children learn boundaries and limits, and gain the self-esteem that is earned from consideration and connection.

Making excuses for our children's behaviors or for their failure to reach certain expectations is very detrimental to their growth as they progress through the school years. There are valid reasons why a student hits bumps in the road academically, athletically, and socially. These are essential to individual growth and development:

1. Making that association between effort and outcome.
2. Realizing that we all have different abilities and therefore a different potential for outcome.

3. Despite great effort, failure can occur, because life is not fair. That is something we need to be sure our children understand, accept, and deal with.

If we make excuses every time the outcome falls short of expectation, we undermine our children's ability to take complete accountability, and we stand in the way of their developing resilience.

This leads to the second part of this chapter: Do not negotiate your child's future. I am appalled at the extent to which parents negotiate their children's future, from applying to private preschools to college entry, from playing time and positions on Little League teams to the same issue on varsity and college teams. Children see through much of this and are left with an empty sense of self—a sense of fulfilling a parent's dream and an absence of the sense of accomplishment that comes from hard work, effort, disappointment, failure, and ultimately earned success.

When my husband and I decided to emigrate from South Africa, we decided very deliberately to move to the USA. We both had developed an abhorrence for entitlement and shared a firm belief that every individual—regardless of family name, tradition, race, religious, or ethnic background—should have the opportunity to succeed through hard work and dedication. We came to the USA with very little. Our experience has been that in most places we have had the joy to live in, there is a respect for the potential of the individual through hard work. I am an idealist who would like to believe that outcome is determined by effort and not negotiation, but I would be naïve to deny that this is always so. One of the most tragic weaknesses of society, groups, families, or individuals today is entitlement: the feeling that one should be automatically given something on a plate, whether it is entrance into private kindergarten, an ivy league education, a place on the Little League traveling team, a membership at certain clubs, or entry into the family business by birthright. The challenge is therefore greater for those who have much, but we should all rise to the following challenge: Do not deprive your children of the gift of having to earn the outcome. Let them own it!

Children who grow up in a privileged environment where parents do not actively focus on accountability, service, and responsibility are at great risk. My best advice to families fortunate enough to have much is to elevate the bar for your children, not in terms of what they can personally accomplish but in terms of what you expect them to contribute to society. In the biblical context, I believe that much will be expected of those to whom much has been given. We have to accept and treasure each of our children for who they are.

At the end of the day our children will only have peace of mind and true contentment if they can look into the mirror and say "I have ownership of who I am; I am content with who I have become; I have used the gifts I have been given the to best of my ability and to contribute back to the greater good."

TAKE-HOME MESSAGES

- Don't make excuses for behavior.
- Give your children ownership of their behavior.
- Teach your children that entitlement is a curse, not a blessing.
- Help your children accept: Life is not fair; deal with it.
- Help your children understand: The more you have been given, the more you owe back to the world.

Risk Failure: Succeed Academically

Supportive, involved, positive parents who partner with teachers give their children the tools to pave their own pathway to academic success. Micromanaging, overzealous parents who are living out their dreams through their children and negotiate their children's path are not only destructive to academic success, but to true success in life.

Rule number one: Allow teachers to be teachers. Parents need to step back and allow the teacher to take the lead. Support the teacher. Offer your child guidance, support, and help with homework, but do not take over as tutor—especially if your child is having academic difficulty. This leads to frustration and a feeling of increased helplessness on the part of the child, who feels pain due to "failing" in front of you. Teachers and tutors are trained professionals. Find the right fit if your child needs extra help and give support and encouragement. Be the "pressure valve"—the one to come to when it is time to let off steam or unload.

Rule number two: Parents, be parents. As parents, it is our role to provide a nurturing, supportive, and structured academic environment. What does that mean? All too often I see parents forgetting the basics and investing time and money in what they consider important (like summer school and private tutoring) without having the basics in place. The child who is nurtured physically and emotionally is much more likely to succeed. Those reassuring hugs (for the good effort even if the grade isn't great), those home-cooked meals, and a family routine that addresses regular sleep and down time are critical. Children know when a test hasn't gone well. They don't need a parent to add to the pressure by pointing out what a disaster it is. Focus rather on the effort that led up to the test and help the child reach reasonable conclusions as to what she might do in the future to help herself.

Rule number three: Know your child. Every child is wired differently and born with different abilities. Every child learns differently. Essentially, we all have a learning difference. It is a great gift when parents and the school treasure the talents of each individual child and help the child overcome relative weaknesses, for we all have areas of strength and relative weakness.

There is nothing more discouraging and counterproductive than merely telling a child to work harder or study longer if he or she just can't "get it."

The analogy I use in my practice to point out the cruelty of such an approach is telling a little one who is paralyzed in a wheelchair to keep trying to walk. The idea is cruel and preposterous, yet the pressures some parents impose academically, without the appropriate support and understanding, are sometimes analogous.

Rule number five: Dispel the myths. The myth of the straight A: It is a tragedy how many parents expect their children to get straight A's or always be on the honor role. It is a tragedy that in many of our schools most of the children who are given straight A's and make the honor role and cannot get passing scores on the standardized tests. The bottom line is an A may be an accomplishment if it is earned and real. If everyone is expected to get As, it means nothing, and your child may be more at academic risk than you realize. One of my little patients said it best "Dr. B, I keep telling my parents that B is for balance, because I'm trying as hard as I can."

The Myth of Praise-Building Self-Esteem

I truly believe that hard-earned, low-key genuine praise does build self-esteem . I believe that easily-come-by, flamboyant, overzealous praise lowers the bar of expectation and cheapens the reward. A quiet and genuine hug has a much greater impact on the child and ultimately the community than a hundred bumper stickers saying "My child get A's" or "My child is a star student." The latter is puffed up and that child may stop performing when the public accolades stop. The child whose quiet sense of self is reinforced with each heartfelt hug and each moment spent with a genuinely proud parent will ultimately be working for success for the right reasons.

The Myth of Advocating for Your Child's Success

Parents confuse being an advocate for their child with negotiating for their child's success. Advocating for your child is putting his or her physical and spiritual wellbeing at the forefront of any action you might take. Negotiating for your children is teaching them to be manipulative. One of the best examples of inappropriate negotiation is the story of a father with a PhD whose first grader brought home a B+ for the first time. The project had involved a title page and a main page, and because she had not followed the directions on the title page, the teacher had appropriately praised her for the project and advised that she needed to follow directions the next time. To those of us with good common sense there are a number of issues that are all too obvious:

1. His daughter is in the first grade.
2. We learn by cause and effect. The simple but important little lesson here is to follow instructions. This will help all through schooling.
3. A B+ in first grade is not the end of the world. It is not a hurricane or family disaster. It has no predictive value for college entry!

The father's response was tragic. He told his daughter how very sorry he was about the B+ (hence sending the message that only As are good enough, and by apologizing, taking inappropriate ownership of her project). He told her that he strongly disagreed with the teacher (hence undermining a wonderful positive influence in her life and losing the value of the lesson on following directions). And he told his daughter that he would go to the school and "fix things." He did, by his definition, though by mine he and his daughter suffered a tragic loss that day. He scheduled time out of his practice and scheduled a conference with the teacher (taking her valuable time out of the classroom) and explained that teacher had destroyed his daughter's self-esteem by giving her a B+. The teacher, patiently explained the importance of this little lesson in the long term and reiterated that this was a small project in the big picture of school life. Sadly, when this irate father threatened "to take things further" the teacher buckled and agreed on a compromise: His daughter could redo the front page and the teacher would re-grade the paper to an A. The tragedy of this is all too obvious. When that B was changed, the balance was lost. His little girl had just learned some very unhealthy lessons:

1. You get what you negotiate, not what you deserve.

2. Deadlines for projects don't mean anything. Your dad can always go back later and get you extra time to get it perfect.

3. Only As are good enough for Dad and he'll do whatever it takes to get them. (Whose project is it anyway?)

When this little girl is in high school, I predict that her dad may proofread, if not type, the final draft of every essay to be sure she gets his A.

Rule number six: Distinguish your role from that of your child's. Help your child discover his own dreams; don't live out your dreams through him. Let me be really specific:

THE PARENTS' ROLE

1. Provide a nurturing, supportive, and safe academic environment.
2. Supply books and project needs in a timely manner, being sure to encourage your child to take the lead in keeping you informed.
3. Partner with the teachers. Be supportive of the teacher when speaking with your child.
4. Have a consistent home schedule.
5. Praise effort and attitude more than the outcome. (I treasure my own parents for the lessons they taught me. Knowing that I was very competitive academically, they always focused on the teacher comments about behavior, effort, and attitude first, saying how important that was to them and how much they loved me. Then in a very low-key way, with unconditional love, they quietly added that they were also proud of my grades. How wise they were.)

WHAT THE PARENTS' ROLE IS NOT

1. Don't DO your child's homework or keep correcting it until it is perfect. The grade belongs to your child, not you, and the teacher needs to be able to identify in what areas your child needs help.
2. Don't make excuses to teachers. (For example, some parents email apologies for homework assignments not done "because Jamie had a social commitment." This speaks for itself.)
3. Don't protect your child from natural conse- quences. Do not try to bail your child out of deten- tion, poor grades, or having to repeat assignments.

YOUR CHILDREN'S ROLE

1. To take ownership and responsibility for their actions from the beginning. This starts with remembering to bring home their flash cards in kindergarten. (Don't drive back to the school after hours for them.) It continues into high school, when planning and executing long-term projects in a timely manner will put them in good stead.
2. To follow behavioral expectations and accept consequences.
3. To get to know who they are, treasure their gifts, and accept and work on their relative weaknesses.
4. To use their gifts, give their best effort, and contribute back to society.

By nurturing, guiding, and supporting your children in a loving manner without micromanaging, you will empower them to take ownership and therefore succeed.

Risk Failure, Succeed Athletically

There are many questions that must be asked and much soul-searching that has to be done when it comes to athletic participation by our children. We have to start by asking ourselves, What is athletic success? Clearly athletic success means different things to different people, and if parents, coaches, and teachers are confused, one can only imagine how confused the children feel. The media coverage over the last years has highlighted outrageous behavior of parents and professional athletes. Concerning the former, there exists the belief that winning (which they define as finishing first) is all that matters. Concerning the latter (professional athletes), entitlement, special privilege, and by and large (with some great notable exceptions) failure to contribute back significantly to society, undermine the accomplishment.

Here are the key questions:

1. What is true athletic success?
2. When should athletic participation begin in childhood?

3. What is the right sport for your child?
4. What is the big picture?

There are a myriad of answers to these questions, and so I will venture my own. I believe that athletic success is when an individual combines the discipline of mind, body, and soul to enjoy to the fullest potential of the athletic activity that they have chosen and to remain well-balanced, contributing individuals.

Note some key issues: Any athletic participation, especially in early childhood, has to be enjoyable and has to be chosen. It is key for parents to know their children and introduce them to a variety of sports and activities so that they develop a love for physical exercise. This is NOT the same as signing them up for every Little league conventional sport in the neighborhood. For the young child, the best sport is backyard or neighborhood play. The Academy of Pediatrics' policy statement is clear about the age- appropriate introduction of organized sports. Parents having fun with their children at an early age is key in the development of a love for exercise. Note, there is much emphasis on the word *fun*. I believe it is detrimental to have an overbearing parent "coaching" a young child in athletic skills and techniques at the age of three! Play and laugh with your child at this age; then play and laugh some more.

Know your child and forget your personal hopes and dreams. You had your chance; focus on your child. I have seen too many little hearts broken when a very athletic father had unrealistic hopes for his uncoordinated, ungainly son, for example. Choose an activity during which your children can feel success and feel good about themselves. For the large uncoordinated child, kicking an oversized soccer ball in the backyard until he builds confidence is of much greater value than signing him up for the competitive neighborhood team, wherein the parents are already focused on their four-year-olds' potential to make the varsity team in high school.

Don't be afraid to wait. The reason second siblings often excel and dare to push the athletic envelope is because they have waited at the sidelines for a couple of years. Waiting is good. Rushing is bad. Hunger for participation is good; it fuels the fire. Don't rush. You risk burnout and loss of zeal!

As your child gets older, in the elementary and middle school years encourage self-improvement. There is an epidemic of private lessons and coaches and children who have everything laid on their shoulders. Remember how many tennis superstars have come from small countries without the huge financial backing and expensive training. Hunger for success cannot be bought, and over-coaching, over-parenting, and micromanaging can send the potentially good athlete in the wrong direction.

Before you sign up to be your own child's coach, evaluate the situation very carefully. Children benefit from positive outside influences in their lives. At least if they strike out and know their coach is disappointed, they have the comfort of knowing that they have two loving, supportive parents in the stands who love them just the same. Remember, don't analyze the reason your child struck out; just give them a hug. The coach will already have given your child feedback. As you evaluate where to sign your children up, avoid political situations. Tragically, they exist even in Little League. The rumors that the coaches' son always get to pitch and that the all-star team is always made up of coaches' sons may be true. You want your children to learn that hard work and determination, as well as using their natural ability, are what is important. Don't let them come away with the message that their future can be negotiated by parental influence or affluence.

When your child does take part in Little League teams, encourage the parents and coaches to keep things low-key.

Focus on healthy fun, laughter, and play at the younger ages. I am saddened by the overkill: huge trophies for all the five-year-olds on the team just for showing up. This definitely lowers the bar of expectation for the future and gives children the wrong motivation to play. This is followed by excessive unhealthy snacks and juices, which tragically contribute to our national epidemic of childhood obesity For reinforcement try a loving hug and beaming smile. Try sliced fresh oranges for the snack and water for the drink. It takes a bit more effort and costs less, and that's part of the point.

There are good lessons to be learned from parents willing to let their children challenge themselves (even if the outcome might not be according to the child's expectations; that is, even if they fail). These lessons can be learned as long as the parents are realistic, encouraging, and supportive.

Mark (age fifteen) wanted desperately to be quarterback on his junior varsity school team. He had dreamed about being quarterback for as long as he could remember and had practiced throughout the summer in preparation for tryouts. His parents knew that although he had potential, there were at least two other boys trying out whose experience and talent were in a league of their own: superior. Wisely, they encouraged Mark to pursue his dream and try out rather than delivering the crushing news: "We just don't think you'll make it. Don't put yourself through this." Also wisely and realistically, they sat down with him before tryouts and lovingly told him, "You will always be our quarterback in our hearts, regardless of what happens tomorrow. But remember that the competition is great, with fine candidates. It is prudent to have a back-up plan—another position you might enjoy playing in case this does not work out." Mark smiled and thanked them but confidently went to tryouts the next day. He was eliminated, and when his parents drove up the slumped shoulders told the story. He felt a quiet comfort while thinking about his parents words from the night before and was relieved that he did not need to shoulder their disappointment as well as his own. (Though their hearts ached for him, they knew that the outcome was fair and that this would be a growth experience.) It took a few days to bounce back, but his parents knew they had raised a fine son when after the first game he said, "Andrew is the finest quarterback a school could have. I'm glad to be able to support him." Mark had learned some of life's most important lessons:

1. It is better to try and fail than never to try at all for fear of failure.
2. It is important to celebrate the success of others (As in Desiderata, "Always there will be greater and lesser persons than yourself.")
3. His parents loved him for who he was and not for what he accomplished.

TAKE-HOME MESSAGES

*   Love of lifelong exercise, health, fun, and balance are the long-term goals.
*   Don't introduce organized competitive sports too early. Exercise through play with little ones, and laugh a lot to make it an enjoyable memory.
*   Allow older children to try different forms of exercise and let them find their own niche.
*   Let the coaches be the coaches.
*   Be supportive, encouraging spectators with impeccable sportsmanship.

CHAPTER 9

Risk Failure: Succeed in Extracurricular Life and Socially

Amy's story was an unhappy one. A wonderful yet shy aspiring actress, she wanted to try out for the lead in the school play. Her parents, concerned that the lead would go to another, persuaded her to withdraw "to protect her from embarrassment." This had been a pattern. Some years later, Amy is still afraid to try anything unless she is sure she will succeed. She remarked last year, "There's that song: 'if you get a chance to sit it out or dance, I hope you'll dance.' Well, I sat it out and I'll never know what it would feel liketo dance." She added, "Even those A+ grades I received for essays...I feel like they weren't really mine. Everything had to be perfect. Mom and Dad would proofread my homework, as if the teacher was grading their grammar, not mine. I remember spending a lot of time on a drama project for my final fine arts grade that was due on a Tuesday morning. I hadn't paced myself well, and although I had completed the rough draft of the play we had to write, I hadn't left enough time to put the final copy into print on my computer. It was after midnight and all my rough draft components were on the floor. I had a calculus test in the morning. My mother took charge (as always): 'Amy, you have to get an A on the calculus exam tomorrow, and this drama assignment should be superb. You know you stand an excellent chance of getting the fine arts prize and others, and the whole family is flying in for honors night. I don't want to be humiliated. You've done the work. I'll stay up and type the final version. You need your rest.' It was always about my mom and living up to her expectations and feeling that her credibility rested on my success. (Failure wasn't an option.) I remember (and always will) making a decision that I would regret. I agreed to let her do it. The grade and teacher comment were the best I'd ever had and I felt sick. When I read the play in its final form, it was perfect. Only it wasn't my work. Firstly I didn't really complete it in a timely manner and I should have planned better. That became a pattern for me when I reached college, as there was no one to bail me out. Secondly there were some subtle changes in the text: punctuation, spelling, etc. Mom sure did a perfect job of 'editing and typing.' The play was chosen to be enacted at the US assembly, and I wanted to hide—especially when the teacher commented that it was the 'fine-tuning' I'd done in the final version that had made the plot even stronger. Our honor code requires that we sign a pledge to say that we never received any help. When I accepted the fine arts prize and when I graduated, I felt a hollow pit in my stomach. I felt lonely and empty. I didn't really know who I was, and the accolades felt hollow. I wish my mom had said, 'Amy, looks like you need to pace yourself better. Explain to your teacher tomorrow that you have fallen behind schedule. It might mean a lower grade, but you will have learned more about how to pace yourself. Besides, I love you just as you are and I'm proud that you tried so hard.' I feel disconnected from my mom because I can't be vulnerable enough to fail. I always wondered if they loved me more because of my performance. My mom's obvious pleasure at my award blinded her to how I felt. Our relationship changed that day. Perhaps the only positive thing to come out of it is I'll never do that to my children, and I won't stand by as a passive accomplice in the future. I am so afraid of college. There is not much I've done on my own."

Amy's story is tragic but poignant. It happens all the time—in school, in extracurricular activities, in life, in relationships. Allow your children to fail and grow. It is a great gift. Don't live through them. That is like placing a noose around their neck.

TAKE-HOME MESSAGES

- If your child has a chance to sit it out or dance, encourage her to dance.
- Our actions model expected behavior for our children more than our words.
- If we are afraid to encourage our children to risk failure, we clip their wings and prevent them from soaring.

Character And Integrity –
The Ultimate Measure Of Success

Character is the stuff of which we are made. It is what we are truly about. It is defined by our actions: trying our best to do what is right even when no one else is looking. It is about choice: what we do with what we have. It is about looking at ourselves at the end of the day and seeking the truth and feeling deep-down contentment and peace because we were true to our conscience.

"The children now love luxury; they show disrespect for elders and love chatter in place of exercise. Children are tyrants, not the servants of their households. They no longer rise when their elders enter the room. They contradict their parents, chatter before company, gobble up dainties at the table, cross their legs and tyrannize over teachers."

Sound familiar? Actually, this was written by Socrates in ancient Greece in about 400 B.C. Let's look at our adult role-modeling of character:

The beginning of the twenty-first century marked the crash of financial icons. CEOs of major public companies were regarded by many as "successful." They were wealthy, with sought-after lifestyles and they crashed because their actions defied integrity and character. The public lessons aren't always easy for children to interpret and learn from. Critical dialogue that is thoughtful, insightful, well informed, and genuine needs to happen between parents, students, teachers, coaches, and community members for children to grow up understanding that integrity and character are important—even in small choices we make—for this is the foundation.

There is an obvious paradox between what is often defined as success and what I believe true success to be. It is to some extent cultural and to some extent at loggerheads with what we reinforce in society as success.

In certain cultures, having stuff is deemed extremely important. People are likely to be described as successful based on the house in which they live, or the car they drive, the salary they earn. There certainly should be no shame in having much. The critical issue for me is that at the end of it all, we will have to face one question: What did I do with what I was given? Therein lies the choice and the true test of whether the individual was successful. That "success" will be defined by the person's character: the choices they made, given the gift of wealth.

Some cultures define success as status: position in society by birthright, career choice, or position of power or authority. Entitlement in any form is a major barrier to the development of character. The greater the responsibility or the authority, the greater the calling to honesty, integrity, and accountability and the tougher the test of character.

Our children learn far more about our own character by observing our actions than by listening to our words. No matter how wise or eloquent we are when we talk to our children, the impact is not only lost but undermined and eroded when our actions are incongruous with our words. The simple act of parking unauthorized in a handicap parking spot may negate all the talking we have done about caring for others and helping those in need. The words become hollow. Encouraging our children to treat others as they would like to be treated and to be patient and kind becomes meaningless if we should skip to the front of the waiting carpool line. Teaching our children about honor and truth is meaningless if we do their homework assignment. Teaching our children to be courteous and polite and show respect becomes meaningless if parents on the sidelines of a Little League game are yelling at the umpire or at each other. These examples sound awful. They happen too often.

Knowledge and accomplishment without character are void. The best lessons in life are learned when we challenge ourselves, fail, and start again with courage and resilience, strengthened by the gift of failure. Allow your children to fail if you want them to succeed.

Bibliography, References, Resources, and Recommended Reading

1. Kindlon and Thompson; Raising Cain (2000)
2. Daniel Goleman; Emotional Intelligence (2006)
3. John Gottman, The Heart of Parenting (1997)
4. Ed Hallowell, The Childhood Roots of Adult Happiness (2003)
5. Wendy Mogel, The Blessing of a Skinned Knee (2003)
6. Robert Coles, The Moral Intelligence of Children (1991)
7. Robert Coles, The Spiritual Life of Children (1991)
8. Michael Gurian, The Wonder of Boys (2006)
9. Michael Gurian, A Fine Young Man (1999)
10. Pollack, Real Boys (1999)
11. Mary Pipher, Reviving Ophelia (2002)
12. Upbringing: Raising Emotionally Intelligent Children (J. Zink)
13. Academy of Pediatrics, Caring for Your Baby and Young Child.(1998)

14. Academy of Pediatrics, Caring for Your Child Aged 5-12 (1998)

15. Academy of Pediatrics, Caring for Your Adolescent Ages 12 - 21 (1991)

16. Mazlish and Faber, How to Talk So Kids Will Listen and Listen so Kids Will Talk (1999)

17. Alvin Rosenfeld, The Overscheduled Child

18. Elkind, The Hurried Child (2001)

19 Stanley Greenspan, Playground Politics (1994)

20 20. Glen Nelson, Raising Self Reliant Children in a Self Indulgent World (

21. E. St James Simplify Your Life

22. Ruth Reardon , Listen To My Feelings

23. Rudolf Dreikurs, Children The Challenge (1991

24. J. Zink The Parents Your Parents Were Not

25. Stanley Turecki, The Emotional Problems of Normal Children (2000)

26. Campbell, How To Really Love Your Teenager (1993)

27. Stanley Turecki, The Difficult Child (2000)

28. Golant and Corwin, The Challenging Child (1995)

29. Mel Levine, All Kinds of Minds (1992)

30. Mel Levine, Developmental Variation and Learning Disorders (1987)

31. Mel Levine, Educational Care (1994)

32. Mel Levine, Keeping a Head in School

Seminars - Conferences - Focus Groups

1. *"Parenting in 2005; Helping Children and Adolescents Survive Their Parents."* Presented by Spencer Gelernter, PhD and moderated by Avril Beckford, MD. FAAP Georgia Chapter Academy of Pediatrics Conference, Fall 2005.

2. *"Parenting Education Resources in Georgia - How Pediatricians Can Promote Better Parenting."* Presented by Martha Rogers, MD, FAAP. Moderated by Avril Beckford, MD. FAAP Ga Chapter Academy of Pediatrics Conference, Fall 2004.

3. *3.."Helping Parents Raise Great Spirits"* Presented by Kenneth Hoats L.P.C . Moderated by Avril Beckford, MD. FAAP Georgia Chapter Academy of Pediatrics Conference, Fall 2003.

4. *"Preventing The Adultification of Sports - Keeping the Sport in Sports."* Presented by David Marshall, MD. Moderated by Avril Beckford, MD, FAAP.

5. *"Book Review - Valuable Resources for Parents."* Presented by Doris Greenberg, MD, FAAP, and Avril

Beckford, MD. FAAP Georgia Chapter Academy of Pediatrics Conference, Spring 2002.

6. *"The Challenge of Combining Parenting and Profession."* Presented by Dr. Michael Popkin, PhD. Moderated by Avril Beckford, MD, FAAP.

7. *"Underlying Mechanisms in Learning and Memory."* Presented by Dr. Kenneth S. Kosik. National Meeting of The Academy of Pediatrics, Fall 2006.

Printed in the United States
63437LVS00006B/37-42

9 781425 976484